Think Like A Dog

How to groom your dog

Kimberly Christian

TABLE OF CONTENT

INTRODUCTION

Your dog will remain clean, healthy, and at ease with regular grooming. Many people prefer utilizing professional groomers because they can keep dogs safe while also making them look fantastic. You may give your dog basic grooming at home, though, if there isn't one close by or you simply want to save some money.

Overall, the grooming experience for the dog should be soothing. If the dog is acting anxiously, the groomer can help by using a soothing, reassuring voice, and there is always the option of taking brief breaks during the grooming session.

Dogs will feel better after a groom, particularly if it has been too long between appointments or if it has been washed repeatedly at home without being dried and brushed through. When not properly brushed or combed after washing, coats have a tendency to tighten up and mat, which will make the dog uncomfortable. This may require that the dog's hair be cut short, as this is the kindest and most comfortable way to relieve the pressure on the coat.

CHAPTER 1 Breeds

However, taking care of a dog can be challenging. Cutting, bathing, clipping, brushing, and cutting a dog's nails can be laborious. You hardly have time to even take care of your dog, let alone yourself! However, it's crucial that you thoroughly groom your pet! Why is this happening, exactly? Simply put, they can't do anything by themselves. You are the only one who can feed, care for, groom, and socialize your dog. So, become familiar with the basics of dog grooming! Here are some simple guidelines for grooming your dog!

You should be aware that a Labrador requires a different maintenance regimen if you previously owned a Spaniel. Different dog breeds require various grooming techniques;

Breed-typical personalities have emerged as a result of several generations of selection for particular qualities. It is possible to predict the potential temperament of a dog by loosely classifying canines based on the work they were bred to undertake. At a young age, breed personalities can be distinguished. Sporting dogs are often intrepid and follow their noses wherever they are led by odors, but they will joyfully come when called by well-known humans. Hounds are typically less interested in human interaction than bird dogs are, and they tend to be more aloof and independent. They are more likely to scout the area on their own and follow a scent or a movement.

Herding dogs have been used for They often assess the situation and begin working on their job. Collie puppies have been observed herding kids, ducklings, or other puppies as a natural expression of their innate inheritance. Even as puppies, guard dogs have a propensity to defend their homes. In order to strengthen their natural protective instincts, dogs bred to guard flocks, like the Maremma or the Kuvasz, are introduced to sheep when they are still puppies. Collies and Akitas have a reputation for being fiercely loyal. Terriers are inclined to be quite aggressive as adults since they were designed to pursue and catch rodents. Collies and Akitas have a reputation for being fiercely loyal. Terriers have a propensity to be incredible qualities that last into adulthood since they were developed to pursue and catch mice. Newfoundlanders are renowned for their ability to save lives.

The ability of a dog to adjust to new circumstances or owners is also influenced by its breed. Dogs cannot be taught such skills. They are inborn—a component of a dog's instinctual behavior—and frequently breed-specific, though mixed breeds have also been noted for having distinctive instincts.

BREED CHARACTERISTICS AND BEHAVIOR IN DOGS

The following behavioral characteristics of several breed kinds are general. These are not intended to be guidelines for conduct. Each dog is unique and has an own personality. This knowledge could be helpful for selecting a dog, comprehending a dog's behavior, and knowing how to groom a dog.

DOGS OF PROTECTION.

The majority of guard dogs were initially bred as herding dogs or flock guardians. Today, we utilize them for a wide range of activities, like as Schutzhund work, police work, house or property security, and specialized sports. Akitas, Rottweilers, and Doberman Pinschers are among the breeds. Mastiffs, Bull Mastiffs, Boxers, Great Danes, and Giant Schnauzers. This group also includes the herding breeds of German Shepherd and Rhodesian Ridgeback, which is employed as a guard, protection, and hunting dog.

A typical behavioral profile includes being confident, in charge, highly trainable, and able to get along with people.

TYPICAL PROBLEMS: Possessiveness, worry over being alone, and aggressive dominance

MOUNTAIN DOGS & FLOCKING DOGS.

Flock guards were developed to secure sheep or cow herds from rapacious predators. To blend in with the flocks, many of them were bred to be white. They often have minimal fear and are quite protective of their families. The Great Pyrenees, Komondor, and Kuvasz are the most well-known in that nation. The St. Bernard, Newfoundland, and Bemese Mountain Dogs are closely related to the flock guards. These creatures have enormous, rounded heads and massive bones, yet they also have a sweet disposition despite being stubborn.

TYPICAL BEHAVIORAL PROFILE: Able to get along well with people, confident, dominant, protective, and independent.

TYPICAL PROBLEMS: Possessiveness, wanderlust, and domineering aggression

HORDOCHING BREEDS

Some people believe that, aside from Northern Breeds, herding dogs retain the most "wolf behaviors." This is because they frequently stalk and pursue (herd). Sheep and cattle are herded by herding breeds. They frequently guard the flock as well. They are typically medium in stature, swift on their feet, sensitive, and able to quickly move the flock with their teeth.

Border Collies are among the breeds. Cole. a Sheepdog from Old England. English Bulldog. Australian Shepherd, three different breeds of Belgian Shepherd. Sheepdog or a heeler. Pull, Bearded Colle, Bouvier, and Sheridan's Sheepdog, among others.

The typical behavioral profile is anxious, domineering, protective, and demanding. sensitivity, loyalty, excellent obedience, and the capacity to get along with people

TYPICAL PROBLEMS: Aggression motivated by fear, separation destructive, nosy Annette

RETRIEVERS...

Whether on land, in the air, or in the sea, retrievers always retrieve. The majority of RETRIEVERS are "party animals," pleasant, gregarious, and extremely energized. The pursuit of the wolf's prey and returning it to the den are two distinct elements for which people have bred. Additionally, these canines must be sufficiently docile to surrender their goods to their humans.

Flat Coated Retriver and Golden Retriever are examples of breeds. Chesapeake Bay Retriever, Curly Coated Retriever. Since they were also employed as property guards, Chesapeake Bay RETRIEVERS are typically less gregarious and outgoing than the other RETRIEVERS and, in fact, may be rather hostile.

TYPICAL BEHAVIORAL PROFILE: Dynamic and in charge. happy. mouthy, loud, excellent in learning commands, and able to cooperate with people

TYPICAL PROBLEMS: During the puppy period, destructive, loud, and mouthy. very effervescent, separation anxiety, sporadic flight or wanderlust, possessive

SPANIELS

Spaniel is derived from the word "Spain," and several members of the group were in fact from that nation. Spaniels are hunting canines that were developed to "spring" or flush wildlife out of bushes. They are popular because they are conveniently proportioned for pets. Pet dogs often only have a lot of hair, or feathering, on their legs and ears. Among the breeds are American Water. Field, Irish Water, English Springer, English Toy, Clumber, Cocker, Tibetan, Welsh, Tibetanian, and Japanese

TYPICAL BEHAVIOR PROFILE: Happy, outgoing, vivacious, "birdy," and loves to fetch things

TYPICAL PROBLEMS include unruliness and possession. destructiveness. mouthy.

Some strains of Cockers and Spnngers are prone to "rage syndrome," a behavioral issue that is assumed to be a type of dominant aggression or even conflict behavior. Without obvious cause, the conduct is characterized by assaulting and biting.

DOGS AS COMPANIONS...

The majority of dogs used as companions are mixed breeds, from Dalmatians to Lhasa Apsos. Anywhere else, they don't quite fit in. The Boston Terrier was originally a friend, the Tibetan Terrier and Lhasa Apso security dogs with some herding thrown in, the Keeshond and Schipperke were barge companions, and the English Bulldog was originally a sporting dog (if you call bull baiting a sport).

Characteristic behavioral profile: ranges from Breeds

TYPICAL PROBLEMS: Dalmatians require a ton of activity and can be aggressive toward people and dogs. The Boston Terrier is tenacious and independent, the Schipperke is extremely dominating and frequently dominantly violent, and the Poodie frequently struggles with separation anxiety and vocal issues.

SETTERS AND POINTERS.

Pointers are extremely vivacious dogs with cheerful and accommodating attitudes. The Dalmatian was once a pointing breed, albeit it only really retains its activity. Setters are hunting dogs as well, and they frequently have a more nervous or sensitive personality. When the Irish Setter was overbred a number of years ago, it lost a lot of behavioral ground.

German Shorthair, Wirehaired and English Pointers, Irish, English, and Gordon Setters are among the breeds.

Both types are characterized by their vivacious personalities. Often anxious, but the majority have pleasant dispositions. good with kids, but lacking in terms of obedience.

TYPICAL PROBLEMS: evading authority, disobeying orders, damaging behavior

DOGS IN FIGHT

While many of these dogs have been developed to be less aggressive. Others still have it, either unintentionally or on purpose. Their violence is largely motivated by their prey-drive, not emotion. Fighting dogs look to be having fun as a result of their wagging tails. Most people are quite independent and obstinate. The sound ones make excellent dogs for kids because they are typically quite devoted to and friendly toward their owners.

Shampei, Pit Bull Terrier, Bull Terrier, Staffordshire and Staffordshire Bull Terrier, and Akita are among the breeds.

A typical behavioral profile might include being active, loving, bonded, predatory, and intense.

TYPICAL PROBLEMS: Unreliable with other dogs or animals, sporadically hostile to people

SCENT HUNTERS.

Scent Hounds, a species with an incredible sense of smell, are master smeliers. The majority of scent hounds have long ears, which can be so long in Bloodhounds and Basset Hounds that they occasionally scratch the ground and stir up more scents. e BREEDS INCLUDE: Otter, Coon, Beagle, Basset, and

TYPICAL BEHAVIORAL PROFILE: Tolerant and sweet-tempered; great with children. hardly bite.

TYPICAL PROBLEMS: Restlessness, sporadic dominance hostility and disregard for instruction

CHAPTER 2 Grooming Techniques

Grooming Your Dog Before The Bath

1 Compile your grooming supplies.

Once you start grooming your dog, you don't want to be searching for your tools. Before you start the task at hand, make sure you have everything you need in one location. To find out what you'll need to groom your dog, refer to the "Things You'll Need" section below.

2 First, comb your dog.

Most mats can be avoided by combing your dog's coat everyday or every other day. For dogs that can mat up, brushing alone is insufficient, contrary to what most literature suggests; the brush will pass over areas where a comb might get caught. The initial phase of grooming should always be a thorough combing because any mats will get tighter.Start with the head first then work your way towards the body. Remember to comb the tail and take care not to scratch the sensitive area under the belly.

- If you come across a tangle when combing, try to untangle it with a brush. Be careful not to overbrush your dog in one area by doing so for an extended period of time. Check if the skin turns red from irritation by peeping underneath the fur.

- Short-haired dogs can be brushed with inexpensive items like curry brushes or gloves.

- Use more specialist tools to comb and brush medium- to long-haired dogs, such as a steel comb, slicker, pin brush, or undercoat rake.

3 Compliment your dog while you brush him.

Reward quiet, composed behavior to promote more of it. You could wish to give the dog a treat as a reward for being well-behaved.

4 Give the canine a break as necessary.

Avoid overwhelming the dog; any bad associations could make future grooming more difficult. Make the experience enjoyable by occasionally giving your pet breaks, giving praise, food, pets, and even engaging in a little bit of play. This will also keep your dog occupied. This is crucial for puppies because they can be trained from an early age to tolerate this kind of handling.

5 Cut away mats that can't be removed by brushing.

When the dog moves, severe matting can pull the skin, making daily life painful for your pet. Depending on how close to the skin it is, you must either cut or shave off a mat if you can't remove it with a brush. If you use scissors, use extra caution to prevent hurting yourself or your pet. To avoid a choppy appearance, try to cut parallel to the direction of hair development.

- Bring your dog to a trained groomer if you don't think you can safely remove the mat without injuring him.

- Sometimes mats can become so snug against the skin that bacterial illnesses develop there. If an infection is suspected Visit the vet as soon as you can with your dog.

- Visual signs of bacterial infection include redness, wetness, and, in more severe cases, pus secretion. Your dog may gnaw or lick the area.

6 Open the canine's eyes.

Breeds with white hair or those with big, watery eyes (Pekingese, Pugs, Pomeranians, etc.) may require more upkeep than others in this area. This procedure might only involve cleaning or removing eye lint from the corners of the eyes, depending on your dog. Dogs with long or white hair may require extra care to ensure that all dirt is removed from the coat because they are more likely to get tear stains. At a pet supply store, you can purchase items designed to remove "tear stains" off a white coat.

- An eye that is healthy should be clear and devoid of any discomfort or unusual discharge.

- Do not attempt to clip your own hair away from the eyes, as Your pet could get hurt. Make the request to your veterinarian or groomer.

7 Clean the ears of your dog.

A clean ear will typically contain some wax, but it shouldn't smell in any specific way. Apply some ear cleaning solution (purchased at a pet supply store) on a cotton round and clean your dog's ears with it. Not too much or the wipe will drip into the ear. Remove debris and wax from the inner ear by wiping; avoid excessively rubbing as this could lead to ulcers. Likewise, avoid getting too close to the ear. Wipe the inside of the ear flag if your dog has drop ears like a basset hound because dirt also builds up there. The general rule for groomers is to just clean what is visible.

- Before applying the ear cleaning solution to the dog's ears, bring it to body temperature. SImIlar to how you would with a baby bottle, submerge it in a body-temperature water bath.

- After cleaning the ear with a damp cotton ball or cloth, gently dry it with another one.

- Reward your dog! He could want some comfort because the ears are a delicate area of the body.

8 If you have ear issues, see a veterinarian.

If your dog's ears appear bloated, red, inflamed, dark, or blackened, they need medical treatment. A call to the veterinarian should also be made if there is any discharge, lesions, or a foul or yeast-like odor. The symptoms of an ear infection that requires treatment include excessive discharge, irritation, one ear that is significantly dirtier than the other, and odor.

9 Clean the canine's teeth

The best way to ensure your dog has healthy teeth and gums is to wash their teeth twice daily with dog toothpaste. Instead of using human toothpaste, use dog toothpaste to avoid fluoridating your dog. Do not try to brush your dog's teeth if there is even a remote risk that you might get bitten by him.

10 If required, get a veterinary cleansing.

A simple dental brushing won't be sufficient if your dog already has a significant accumulation of tartar and plaque. Your dog needs a professional cleaning at the vet's office, just like a human would. There is also the option of teeth cleaning without anesthetic, which veterinarians normally do not provide.

- Look for red gums or brown substance stuck to the teeth as these are indications that your dog will experience pain during at-home tooth brushing. Before you try to brush his teeth, take him to the vet.

11 Trim the canine's nails.

Uncut dog nails can cause joint damage by curling under into the paw pads or twisting the toes. Depending on how quickly your dog's nails grow, trim them frequently to maintain them short. His nails are excessively long and touching the ground if you can hear them clicking on the floor as he walks.

- With a pair of dog nail clippers, remove a very tiny portion of the nail (1/16 inch). For a small dog or very young puppy, human clippers are acceptable. Scissor-style clippers are more efficient than guillotine-style clippers. Use clippers that are the right size for your dog.

- If your dog has clear nails, you can see the blood vessel-containing pink portion (the quick). Do not clip the pink portion; only the clear, firm nail should be trimmed.

- Be extremely cautious not to clip dark-nailed dogs' nails too short (blood vessel). Go slowly and just remove a small portion at once. Dremeling, which only removes a tiny amount of material at a time, is significantly safer and makes it simpler to prevent cutting yourself.

- Apply styptic powder, cornstarch, or flour with a little pressure and hold for a few seconds to stop any bleeding if you make a too-deep cut and strike a blood artery.

- This is the worst part for the majority of dogs. Some people complete this procedure last to prevent the dog from becoming overly anxious and incapable of performing much grooming thereafter. You can wash simply the paw with some water or wipe it clean with hydrogen peroxide to get the blood off after applying blood clotting agents if you clip your nails last and quickly the nail.

Bathing your Canine

1 Compile your materials.

Have everything ready before you begin so that you don't have to scramble to find cleaning supplies while a wet dog is in the tub. Additionally, you should wear appropriate clothing that you don't mind getting dirty because you will get wet. You will need:

- puppy shampoo

- Treats

- several towels

To prevent water from splashing over the side of the tub, place one towel there. The rest are used to dry things.

2 Put a non-slip material on the tub's bottom.

You are aware from previous experience that the tub might get slippery after being soapy. Put a blanket or non-slip bath mat in the tub to stop your dog from slipping.

3 Start a lukewarm shower.

In particular if your dog has short hair, hot water might damage their skin. Running water on the dog immediately away could create unnecessary stress and burns if it begins to get too hot without first checking. Your dog may need some time and his favorite goodies to get desensitized to the sound of running water.Use a hose outside to clean your dog if you just have a tub and no shower since using a cup to drench your dog in water or a tub full of water to totally soak him in water may leave him with dry skin and an infection. This is valid for even dogs with short hair, such as pit bulls; you only need to use a hose's low power setting so as not to harm or overstimulate the dog while still getting the job done.

- Because some shampoos have special dilution recommendations, read the shampoo's directions carefully. If you are unable to locate such instructions, use the product exactly as is since excessive dilution may compromise the dog's cleanliness

- Some shampoos should not be used for a regular bath because they are only meant to treat fleas and ticks; they are not meant to prevent them.

4 Lock the canine inside the bathtub.

When it's time for a bath, some dogs like to flee. Purchase a dog bath lead from the pet supply store if this applies to your dog. It is a leash that holds your dog securely during the bath thanks to a suction cup attachment to the shower wall.

- Change the dog's ordinary collar for one that won't damage the coat or absorb moisture. The ideal lead is a slip lead that adapts to a straining dog, but no matter the restriction, the dog may choke on itself, so be sure to watch his respiration and make adjustments or merely push them back as needed.

5 Give your dog a good soak.

Before you begin shampooing your dog, make sure the coat is completely wet. You can purchase and use a hose and water pressurizer attachment for the faucet if your dog isn't terrified of it. If you have a large dog or one with a double coat, this is extremely useful. RESIST the urge to put water in your dog's ears. An infection may result from water in the ears. Please be careful to only spray or rinse the dog's neck with water. You may clean the head independently.

6 Give the dog a bath.

Start at the neck and work your way down toward the back and legs, spreading the shampoo with your fingers as you go. Avoid using soap near the ears and eyes and save the head for last (unless you have tearless shampoo meant for dogs). Instead, wash the head with a moist washcloth or towel.

- Running a rake or rubber curry brush through a double-coated dog's coat after shampooing will help to loosen it and improve shampoo distribution. Just be careful not to rake one area for an extended period of time.

- If shampoos are correctly diluted, they could be simpler to use and rinse off.

7 Give your dog a good rinse.

Continue rinsing as long as you notice dirt or soap bubbles in the water flowing off of a particular region. You can apply the same technique you used to shampoo the dog's coat after soaking it. There are vets who can administer the right amount of sedation—not too much—to allow you to groom your dog in a couple of hours or who can groom the dog themselves if it is too fearful of running water or baths in general and you are unable to do it yourself. Touch the dog all over to check for shampoo, paying special attention to the difficult-to-reach areas between the legs and the chest. Rub the fur between your fingers and gently tug to see whether it's clean.

8 Dry Your Canine

To remove water from the coat and body, use a squeegee or your hand as one. So that you don't make a mess, try to towel-dry him as much as you can while he's still in the tub. If you want to allow your dog to shake the water off their body, place the towel over his back or hold it close to him. Many dogs pick up on the "bath rules" and learn to hold off on shaking until you have draped a towel over them to catch any drips. A chamois, which resembles a thin fleece towel and is intended to be wrung out when wet, is another option for a towel to be used. The amount of towels required is reduced, and the majority of work is reduced.

9 If required, blow dry the dog.

Blow-drying can dry the coat without overheating or over-drying your dog if towel-drying is insufficient. If your dog's hair is particularly long, you might need to dry the coat as you brush it. The quickest option is towel drying followed by blow drying.

- Ensure the blow dryer is set to the cool setting! There will be less of a possibility that your dog's hair and skin will dry out, so even though it might take longer than normal, it will be worth it.

- Don't push your dog if he reacts negatively to the blow dryer's sound or sensation. Dry him off with a towel as much as you can, then place him somewhere where he can't get wet.

Haircutting Your Dog

1 Determine whether you should trim your dog's coat.

Many breeds have short hair, thus frequent cutting is not necessary. However, if your dog is a shaggier breed, regular cutting might be necessary for his health. Cocker spaniels, sheepdogs, poodles, collies, Shih Tzus, Pekingese, and chow chow are a few of the breeds that require routine coat trims.

2 After the dog's fur has completely dried, trim it.

If you intend to trim the hair on your dog, be careful to read the clippers' instructions. For advice on how to use your clippers correctly, purchase an informational book or DVD or speak with a groomer. Make sure the clippers are properly oiled and that the blades are sharp. The blades may pull on the hair if they are not sharp.

You should have a concept of the aesthetic you want to achieve before trimming your dog. For information on how to accomplish the desired result, read, research, and watch videos. Then you can begin.

3 Gently restrain the dog.

Tie him up with a leash if you don't want him to be moving around. Your spare hand can be positioned beneath the dog's tummy to encourage him to remain still while having his nails clipped. Continue to praise the dog while remaining calm, even sing to him. Having healthy treats is also a wonderful idea.

4 Use dog clippers for grooming.

Investing a little bit more money in a quality set of dog grooming clippers is worthwhile. You won't have to hire specialists to groom your pet, thus a small investment now will save you money afterwards.

- Use dog grooming tools that will result in the desired coat length.

- With scissors, you won't likely get a smooth, even coat, and if the dog moves unexpectedly, you risk injuring him. It's advised to use grooming clippers rather than scissors.

5 Trim the dog's fur carefully.

As long as you don't firmly press the blade into the skin, you can place the blade against the body without risk. Before running the clippers in the other way—with the direction of hair growth—backbrush against the direction of hair growth. With the exception of leaving a shorter length than the clipper blade you are using, utilizing the clippers against the growth of hair will have the same effect as back-brushing. A blade size decreases by two blade sizes when shaving against the direction that the hair is growing. Check how long a 7# leaves behind while cutting with the grain when using a 4#, for instance. Move the clippers gently but with precision. Too much speed could result in crooked lines. Unless you want the hairs to be shorter than the blade says it will leave, always move the blade in the direction that the hairs develop. Start at the neck and work your way down to the shoulders, behind the ears, and then in the direction of the chin, throat, and chest regions.

6 Exercise caution when shaving the area surrounding the anus.

The anus might unintentionally pop out like a button and be mistakenly cut as a result. Run the clippers only outward from the anus and under the base of the tail, never over it. Use your clippers like you would a pencil.

- When trimming the legs, tail, and face, take care. These places might be delicate. The dog will also avoid obstacles and can wind up cutting itself from jerking too quickly.

- Make sure the clippers are never hot enough to harm your dog's skin by checking them periodically. If the clipper blades do become hot, stop using the machine and spray some "Clipper Lube" on them

7 Praise your pet.

It can be challenging to remain still! Give your dog a break every few minutes if it appears like all this handling is wearing him out. Throughout the procedure, compliment him and offer him snacks. Avoid playing with the dog in situations where he might become muddy or become too eager to remain still during the activity again.

8 Take it slow.

Before you get a clean, even cut, you might need to go over your dog's coat several times. Do not rush! Give your dog as many breaks as need, and cut your dog's hair slowly. To get a smooth cut, brush up against the coat and then go over the area with clippers one more. Before you finish, you will need to do it numerous times.

CHAPTER 3 Do's and Don't

Do's

1. Regularly groom.

Do you own a long mane? It would be awful if you neglected to wash and comb it for weeks or even months. You might not immediately detect some dogs' uncomfortable matting and skin issues. Pomeranians and

Shih Tzus are two breeds that require frequent brushing. Regular nail trimming is also recommended for dogs. The health of dogs can be endangered by overgrown nails, and cutting overgrown nails can cause unnecessary stress and discomfort for your dog. Dogs are far less inclined to cooperate when they are unhappy.

2. Show patience.

Dogs are sensitive to tension, so be mindful of your own state of calm and relaxation as well as the amount of time you've allocated for the grooming session. Move slowly and concentrate on your actions and your dog's response.Take a break if necessary and keep an eye out for symptoms of stress, such as trembling, whining, or panting that isn't caused by the heat. When using scissors and nail clippers, use particular caution. Try grooming more frequently, like once a week, and simply do a tiny bit at a time if your dog has a tendency to panic and won't stay still. If necessary, only trim a few nails at a time when trimming your dog's nails. And don't forget to shower him with attention, affection, and treats. Make it a successful endeavor. Your dog will ultimately become accustomed to the procedure and feel more at ease if you are polite and patient with them.

3. Pick a place that is secure and well-lit for grooming.

In order to prevent Fido and Bella from slipping and falling, you need to be able to see what you're doing and have a safe, nonslip surface. When grooming your dogs, avoid tethering them because this might cause severe mishaps. Of course, if they enjoy being brushed, give them as many brushes as you can—this may be a wonderful way to strengthen your relationship. Even when they don't enjoy a certain grooming method, you can utilize brushing as a reward.

4. Make use of the right tools for grooming dogs.

Are you using the proper brush when you brush? A specialized brush can be required depending on the type of fur and skin on your dog. Learn more about the best type of brush online or from your veterinarian.Make sure your dog's nail clippers, scissors, trimmer, etc. are all of high quality and suitable size. Never be afraid to seek advice from your veterinarian if you're unsure.

5 Keep in mind that breeds with long hair or double coats need a lot of upkeep.

The adage "length hair don't care" is not applicable to dogs. These dogs can easily get mats on their bodies if they aren't brushed frequently, including behind their ears, behind their front legs, and in front of their hind legs. Check your dog's coat frequently. Before clipping their nails, dogs with lengthy fur on their paws may benefit from having that cut.

6 Recognize your limitations.

Your dog might resist being calm and still while being groomed despite your best efforts and intentions. If this occurs, think about asking a trustworthy friend to assist you with grooming, or ask your veterinarian about taking natural sedative supplements.

Don't

1. Be patient.

Would you appreciate it if your nail tech or hair stylist was rushing? No. Bella wouldn't either, sadly. Ask PetSmart, hurried grooming can lead to stress and even life-threatening blunders.

2. Refrain from grabbing Fickle by his fur.

This should never be used during grooming, just like tethering.

3. Avoid using perfumed shampoo.

Dogs' sensitive skin and nostrils might become irritated by perfumed bath products. Select a fragrance-free shampoo, such as this one from 4 Legger.

4. Avoid giving your dog frequent baths.

Only bathe Bella when absolutely necessary, such as after she has rolled in something and gotten filthy or smelly. Bathing dogs can dry out their skin and interfere with their ability to regulate their body temperature. Make sure your dog gets a warm bath because taking a bath in cold weather might lower a dog's body temperature. Always use a towel to dry your dog; a blow dryer can scare dogs and make them overheat.

5. Avoid trying to do too much at once to avoid exhausting your dog.

Avoid the error of attempting to fit all of the tasks on your dog's grooming checklist—a wash, fur clipping, nail trimming, toothbrushing, and other tasks—into a single session. Instead, break up grooming duties into fewer, more frequent periods. Do not wait until your dog is agitated or stressed before concluding each session on a positive note. You want Fido to say, "That was fun," as he leaves.

6. Avoid trimming nails too short.

Even the calmest dog may become agitated when nails are trimmed too short because it hurts. The "quick" blood vessel can be found in dog nails. Cutting into the quick can cause intense pain and blood. The quickest solution is to just trim the nail tips off more frequently. Simply cut your dog's toenails if they develop "hooks." Never attempt to cut Bella's nails when she is agitated; always wait until she calms down. Try clipping just one nail at a time if your dog finds nail-trimming very upsetting.

7. Never use a guard with nail clippers.

Some dog nail clippers have a protection built in to stop over-trimming, but the drawback is that it will obstruct your vision. Cut Fido's nails while his paws are resting on a hard surface, like the floor or a table, or use your finger as a protection instead. This will serve as protection. Buy high-quality clippers, please.

8. Forget to wash your dog's ears.

Use only Q-tips as directed by your veterinarian. In order to avoid painful ear infections, clean your dog's ears sometimes if necessary using an ear cleaner. Ask your veterinarian for a recommendation or try this ear cleaner from Halo. Just keep in mind to avoid getting your dog's ears wet while bathing. Infections in the ears from water and shampoo can be painful and deadly.

9. Neglecting your grooming supplies.

Blades for toenail clippers should also be sharpened frequently and changed at least once every few years. In addition to not cutting efficiently, dirty or dull blades can strain and tug at your dog's nails.

10.   Not trying.

It may take some time for you and your dog to feel comfortable grooming at home, but that's okay. However, if you believe that your pet needs to be professionally groomed, pick a local groomer who comes highly recommended. Preferably, choose a mobile grooming service that, if possible, can groom your dog at home. Read reviews and ratings to learn more about your alternatives. Ask your veterinarian for a referral if you're unsure. Additionally, confirm that the groomer you select will let you keep your animal partner with you while it is being groomed. Keep in mind that you are your dog's strongest supporter and defender.

CHAPTER 4.   Proper Tools Needed

Starter Tool Kits Must Contain:

- **Direct Shear**

- bent shear

- Shear Pin Brush for Thinners

- Slicker Soft Brush

- Combination Rubber Curry and Shampoo Brush Comb

- Pet Rake

- Matting Remover

- Cutters for nails

- Curved Locking Professional Animal Clipper Hemostats (Andis, Oster, Wahl)

- Stick Brush

- Slicker Soft Brush

- Rubber shampoo/curry brush and deshedding tool

- Blending Comb

- Pet Rake

- Matting Remover

- Cutters for nails

- nail clippers

- Curved Locking and Dematting Tool for Hemostats

- Spiking Powder

- An ear cleaner

- ear cream

- Shampoo

- **Conditioner**

- **Face wash**

- **Wipes**

- **Fragrance fritz**

CHAPTER 5 General Care

Responsible pet ownership starts with providing for pets properly. Understanding that you are making a lifetime commitment to a furry family member who needs on you for their health and well-being is crucial when adopting a pet.

Fortunately, the unconditional love and happiness that pets bring into our lives more than make up for the extra responsibility that comes with bringing a furry kid into your household. The following are the requirements that all responsible pet owners must fulfill in order to ensure your pet's health and happiness.

Pets require wholesome food.

Pets need food that satisfies their unique nutritional requirements, just like people do. The nutritional requirements of a dog are met by dog meals, and those of a cat are met by cat foods. Importantly, they have quite different food requirements. Different diet is needed for puppies and older dogs. Special diets may be necessary for pets with health conditions. The majority of the foods we eat, like salt, garlic, and onions, are bad for your pet's health and can make them sick or even be fatal. As a result, dogs and cats should generally avoid eating table scraps.

Pets should receive the appropriate amount of food, too. Obesity may result from overfeeding or over rewarding your pet, which may ultimately cause other health issues, including heart disease, kidney issues, and others.

To prevent these illnesses, weigh your options when it comes to pet food. If you're unsure of which foods would be best for your pet, it's a great idea to ask your veterinarian for advice.

Give your pets access to clean water at all times.

Pets require easy access to water to survive, just like humans do. All animals in your care should always have access to a clean, fresh dish of water. Place it nearby their meal bowl to make it more convenient, and don't forget to replenish your pet's water dish at least twice daily. As a result, your pet will stay cool, hydrated, and healthy. Clean aquariums at least once a week if your pet, such fish or turtles, lives in water.

Providing a secure, comfortable home for pets is part of proper pet care.

Cats are constantly at risk from predators, violent dogs, and cars, so keeping them inside is in their best interest.The ability to hide and feel protected in a covered section of their home that resembles a cocoon is something that many cats value.

If you allow your dog go loose in your fenced-in yard without a leash, be sure he is microchipped, wearing identification tags, and that your contact information is up to date and the microchip is registered. Additionally, registering your pet with Finding Rover is a smart move.Shelter and water should always be accessible. Older dogs, in particular, may benefit from having an orthopedic dog bed indoors because they often appreciate having their own bed.

Regular potty breaks are necessary for pets.

A variety of animals can be trained to use the bathroom in a house without worrying about accidents. At least one litter box should be available for cats.

Every one to two hours during the day, puppies typically need to go potty. A puppy can typically hold it for as many hours as she is old in months plus one. For instance, a three-month-old puppy needs to go potty at least once every four hours. You'll discover what your own dog requires, but a dog doesn't need to "hold it" for a minimum of six hours. Similar to elderly adults, senior dogs also need to go potty more regularly. It is possible to train dogs to use potty pads, doggie doors, or to wait until they are taken for a walk before going potty. In any case, make sure to clean your pet's bathroom frequently. In order to keep filth and bacteria from building up and endangering your pet's health, practice good hygiene and sanitation. Having a spotless space for your pets to use would be very helpful.

Make sure your animal companion exercises frequently.

Exercise is an essential component of proper pet care. Exercise is crucial for both the physical and mental health of your pet. If you spend any time on social media, you probably already know that all kinds of animals enjoy playing, like this turtle who is bouncing a ball, this dog who is playing fetch by himself, or this bird who is playing with a red cup. Some people mistake what they see as a pet's misbehavior for the animal simply being bored and amusing itself by getting into the trash, destroying the couch, or, well, you get the idea.

Whether it be through regular interaction with you, having visitors over, or going on outings, pets can benefit from socialization. to broaden their horizons and enhance their interpersonal abilities while enabling them to try new things in a secure manner!

Healthy behaviors and healthcare appointments are necessary for pets.

You should bring your pets in for wellness examinations at least once a year to make sure they are strong and agile.

The wellbeing of your pet is also significantly influenced by clean teeth and healthy gums. Take your pet to the veterinarian or animal hospital as soon as you see any sickly signs or symptoms so they can start feeling well as soon as possible.

Regular grooming is another way to keep your pets happy and healthy (if needed). For dogs, matted fur can be uncomfortable and unhealthy. Although washes, brushings, nail trimmings, and flea/tick removal may be required for your pet's health, dogs and cats may not enjoy it.

CONCLUSION